Bighorn petroglyphs, Basketmaker Culture, Monument Valley Navajo Tribal Park, Arizona.

ART
on the
ROCKS

including
STONE WONDER
An Introduction to the Rock Imagery of the Southwest
by
BRUCE HUCKO

SIERRA PRESS
Mariposa, CA

Snake petroglyphs, Pueblo IV Culture, northern New Mexico.

PHOTO ©WILLIAM STONE

The Quail Panel, pictographs, Basketmaker Culture, southeast Utah.

BRUCE HUCKO

Indian rock art comes in two forms. Petroglyphs are images pecked, stippled, ground, incised, abraded, and scratched into the rock. They are found on rock surfaces, cliffsides, and boulders coated with "desert varnish," a stain composed of iron and manganese oxides. Pictographs are colored rock paintings and drawings made with a variety of mineral dyes. They occur on canyon walls, boulders, and rock shelters where they are protected from weathering. Rock art is commonly found in river corridors and their tributary canyons. Settings range from dwelling interiors and near building sites to lofty, difficult-to-reach surfaces.

STONE WONDER

by Bruce Hucko

THE SLICKROCK CANYON CURVES STEEPLY UP, an ancient serpent cutting its form into a sand dune now turned to stone. Sheer walls of cross-bedded sandstone stand as guardians. I enter the canyon and am home. Slickrock is my foundation, my ceiling the azure sky.

Today I hike alone so that I can give my complete attention to the land. I have no agenda. Just being in the landscape satisfies me. Anything else is just frosting on the cake of life. My first gift is at my feet. A small potsherd, black-on-gray, lies nestled in the sandy arroyo. Without picking it up I stand and turn a slow circle, looking all around me. I am once again reminded that I am not alone, that I am walking in country that's been lived in for a very long time. It's a feeling you wear like a favorite flannel shirt.

Several hours later and miles into the country, tired and gritty, I turn the last corner in the canyon. A sandstone ramp angles sharply up to the right. It appears broad enough to walk on. My feet are leery. My body whines, "Stay low, it's easier," but something stronger, more intuitive says, "Go this way." I have learned to listen when serendipity calls.

Near the top a familiar force turns my head toward the cliff wall, which reaches several hundred feet up to the sky. Behind a jumble of boulders at its base, some 50 yards away, I see the nearly hidden image of an animal. My heartbeat quickens. An adrenal surge straightens my back. I am smitten with joy.

I put down my pack in the sparse shadow of a juniper. Carefully stepping stone to stone I am able to reach the site without disturbing the soil crust that covers the ground in front of me. "Leave No Trace" is a game I play while hiking.

I am astounded by what I see. A line of figures pecked into the rock above a horizontal crack move right to left toward a large spiral. More figures come toward the spiral from the other side. Some carry crook-necked staffs, some appear to carry burden baskets, but most are just walking. No water bottles, no fanny packs, no camping gear. These unfettered figures are joined by an array of large animal figures, bighorn and deer. Above this scene several large anthropomorphic figures, bodies etched with curved lines and dots, peer down on the landscape with large, open eyes.

Leaning against the boulders I gaze upon the panel as though it were a movie screen, a sandstone Eye-Max! Before I can relax, the voices of friends and books wanting to explain it all stampede my heat-crazed, interpretation-imperiled brain. This is not the cliché chant of an ancient medicine man backed by an Indian flute. No! It's that inexplicable madness of culture that drives me to make some practical meaning to all of this. What is going on here?

The recording of significant events, thoughts, and religious experiences is a distinctly human characteristic. The ancient wanderers of this land recorded hunting scenes, astronomical events, and their own migratory processions. The coming of the horse is depicted in many panels and is usually signified by helmeted Spanish riders. Ute rock art from the 1950s depicts government officers arriving in Mancos Canyon to take children to distant schools. Historic Navajo rock art depicts military equestrians, cars, and other modern scenes. The Hopi continue to record their religious pilgrimages to the Grand Canyon.

OPPOSITE: Procession Panel, petroglyphs, Basketmaker Culture, BLM, Utah.
PHOTO ©BRUCE HUCKO

I want to rid myself of this self-indulgent, analytic mind and allow the lines, colors, and shapes to caress the hidden cavities of my thoughts, the untended gardens of understanding that require nurturing from images such as these to survive. But not yet. The voices rave and I sit paralyzed by the sound of it all. Brazen attendant voices shout over my shoulder.

"It symbolizes the return to the spirit world."

"It's like a traffic counter telling who went this way."

"Those aren't staffs, those are snakes they're holding."

"What's for lunch?"

More than any other element of ancient Southwest culture, rock art seems to invite the greatest range of speculation and interpretation. Books, calendars, coffee cups, and T-shirts are emblazoned with ancient imagery. We all think we know what they are saying, but do we? Cast onto our minds like wild seed these enigmatic images challenge us to find a reason for their existence. Something innately human calls forth from the rock beckoning us to seek its meaning. And when we can't read the ancient story we create our own.

The original artists are long gone, metamorphosed into the landscape where they are no longer available for interviews. What would they say of our efforts to decipher them? "Good of you to be considering our work so sincerely, yet silly of you to be taking yourselves as seriously as you do." I hear their laughter on the wind and in Raven's mocking cry.

Shieldbearers, petroglyphs, Pueblo IV Culture, Galisteo Basin, New Mexico. PHOTO ©MARY ALLEN

All American Man, pictograph, Pueblo II-III Culture, Canyonlands National Park, Utah.

PHOTO ©BRUCE HUCKO

Shieldlike designs, often with protruding head, hands, and feet, are frequently found on the Colorado Plateau and along the Rio Grande. Shields and other roundish designs appear in late Pueblo II-III rock art (post-AD 1000) and continue to the historic period. They usually occur as individual elements and are often found near cliff dwellings. Their highly visible locations and bold designs suggests that they functioned as signposts. They may have identified groups occupying the dwellings. Today at Hopi, shields are used to represent the masks of deities and katsinas. Pueblo Indians incorporate shields in several dances. The Ute, Apache, and Navajo all have traditional uses for shields.

Spiral petroglyph, Hohokam Culture, Signal Peak, Saguaro National Park, Arizona.

Spiral solstice marker, petroglyph, Basketmaker Culture, BLM, Utah.

PHOTO ©BRUCE HUCKO

The universal spiral form appears in many rock art panels. Its circular form suggests increasing knowledge and is often associated with pathways of the mind, heart, and spirit. Each modern Indian culture reads spirals in its own way. Hopi and Zuni stories tell of of "finding the Center," of spiraling inward in the search for peace. To them a spiral is a sort of spiritual "map." The Navajo migration story is often simply represented as a spiral moving up and out from the place of emergence. Spirals are often found at archaeoastronomical sites, where they work in conjunction with elements of light and shadow to mark seasonal changes.

Deer, elk, bear, and a variety of birds can be found pecked and painted on rock surfaces throughout the Southwest. Insects, turtles, and lizardlike beings abound. Along the San Juan River are anthropomorphs with ducklike heads. Animal presence in rock art indicates the dependence that ancient peoples had on them. Animals fed the people and gave them the materials to make moccasins, clothing, tools, weapons, jewelry, and ceremonial implements. Present-day Indian cultures speak of these things as gifts. Animals are respected and honored in dance, song, and ceremony among all southwestern tribal people today.

Deer petroglyph, Basketmaker Culture, Behind-the-Rocks WSA, BLM, Utah.

PHOTO ©BRUCE HUCKO

OPPOSITE: Duck Head Man, petroglyph, Basketmaker Culture, Glen Canyon NRA, Utah.
PHOTO ©BRUCE HUCKO

STONE WONDER
—Part Two—

SEVERAL ELDERS FROM SAN JUAN PUEBLO MAKE THEIR WAY among an array of boulders near the banks of the Rio Grande. Gray haired and walking slowly the group looks aged but acts much younger. Smiles gleam on furrowed faces as they turn and face one of the boulders. On its darkly patinated surface is carved a man carrying a shield. Next to it a horned animal plays the flute. Silently and deliberately each elder brings forth a small bag of cornmeal. While prayers are muttered each of the elders lightly scatters this symbolically sacred substance on the rock.

The elders then turn to instruct the children who have traveled with them to this hillside full of carved images. "Say what's in your heart. You are talking to the spirit of your ancestors." Some of the children giggle, but most stare with wide-eyed wonder at the imagery before them and listen intently to the words of their elders, their grandparents. "This is our history book," says one of the women. "What you read at school is the history of the world, of all people. This is the history of our Tewa people, yours and mine."

All of the children take cornmeal and make their offering. A few just toss it toward the stone. Others seem to be saying something to themselves before letting the cornmeal trickle between their fingers. Two have moved away from the group and found their own image to speak to. The Tewa term *seda* refers to the people who made the marks and the marks themselves. They are as one.

Native Americans who recognize themselves as descended from these ancient image makers respond to rock art in a poignantly different way from the rest of us. Their model provides insight for us all.

Hopi people recognize that they have long been part of the southwestern landscape. The Hopi recognize rock art imagery from Casas Grandes, Mexico, to the Valley of Fire, Nevada, and from central Utah to the Sonoran Desert. It holds the land together like a spider web and tells them their place in it.

The Hopi Office of Historic and Cultural Preservation speaks of the "markings in stone" as "... footprints. They mark where we came from and according to our stories, they will one day lead us back to those places. Our understanding of them is imbedded in our language. To us the markings are more than art for they are spiritually and culturally alive. We are concerned that our meaning and interpretation are often miscommunicated. It's a difference of intellect and culture."

The Navajo call rock art *tse' kisnaascha*, "images created onto the rocks." They say that when the Holy People decided it was time to no longer live among the Navajo as physical beings they turned to the rocks and cast their images upon them, thereby leaving the Navajo people with their final prayers, songs, and guidance for living imprinted on the land. When viewed "that moment in time lives again."

The Navajo speak of having always been here. The presence of recognizable rock art images in Dinetah—the place of emergence, Canyon de Chelly, and throughout Navajoland is their evidence.

Fertility is a theme that unites all rock art imagery. Like their present-day descendants, the ancient people of the Southwest seemed to be aware that they were but one member of the community of life. They knew that Earth, as mother, gave birth to all life equally. That relationship with the forces of nature is celebrated in their art. Birthing scenes, plant life, animal life, hands, and human forms are frequently in proximity. Discussions with native elders reveal that even abstract circles, dots, and lines can be read as part of the ever-present, Mother Earth concept.

OPPOSITE: Birthing Rock, petroglyph, Fremont Culture, BLM, Utah.
PHOTO ©BRUCE HUCKO

Back among the Tewa elders I learn a good lesson. "That looks like someone carrying a shield," I say about the round figure decorated with circles and lines with an obvious head, legs, and arms showing. "No," says my elderly companion softly, "it's the pueblo. That person is holding it." After a short pause she adds, "maybe it's both." Here, knowledge is gracefully delivered. Leave an opening for what you don't now know or readily understand, whether it comes from another person or a force beyond your immediate understanding.

No one can say with certainty what the images mean, what they were used for. Present-day American Indian people, generations removed from those who made the rock art, are cautious when speaking of it, for many images are considered sacred and speaking of them out of context can be dangerous. Though much of the culture of the past is alive today in native stories and ceremonial practices, more has been lost or changed over time.

What holds is that the painted and pecked images of past peoples still live in the lives and cultures of all tribal people leading modern lives in the desert Southwest. The primary concern of all of these people is that the imagery and the cultures related to them be treated with respect.

When I asked Acoma poet Simon Ortiz to define the Keresan language term for "ancestral People," he spoke for minutes in his native tongue. Imbedded in his linguistic connection were concepts of "sacred evidence" and "those long-ago people to whom we are all connected." "*All*," says Ortiz, "meaning not just indigenous people, but all people of the world." With this in mind the relationship between myself and the imagery on this stone wall becomes more intimate. If I acknowledge the connection, then respect is there.

Fluteplayers, petroglyphs, Basketmaker Culture, BLM, Utah.

Fluteplayers and rainbows, pictographs, Basketmaker Culture,
Canyon de Chelly National Monument, Arizona.

PHOTO ©FRED HIRSCHMANN

One commonly recognized image is the flute-player, mistakenly called Kokopelli. In fact, Kokopelli is part of the Hopi katsina tradition and is concerned with fertility. He is often portrayed with a large phallus and wears a pack, supposedly filled with fertile seeds. Only on occasion does he carry a flute. The humpback flute-player is different, although there are parallels in symbolism. They appear in varied form—slender, hunched, humped, lying down, standing, single, grouped, and usually in the company of other figures. They almost always appear to be actively playing. Though most are of human form, flute-playing animal and birdlike figures exist as well.

Abstract panel of pictographs, Archaic Culture, southern New Mexico.

LAURENCE PARENT

Abstract cloud design, petroglyph, Jornada Mogollon Culture, Three Rivers site, New Mexico. PHOTO ©WILLIAM STONE

Squiggles, lines, dots, circles. Occurring in both paintings and petroglyphs, abstract rock art imagery suggests plants, insects, bird tracks, playground equipment, paws, people, and other ideas. Archaic hunters and gatherers who roamed the desert Southwest from approximately 5500 BC to AD 1 were the greatest practitioners of this art form. Theirs is also the earliest recorded rock art, and perhaps that is why it appears abstract: they were just beginning to explore the medium and their minds were better adapted to coding their experience in a nonlinear way. Seemingly playful and naive, the meaning of these images may be quite profound. If only we could interview the artists!

Bighorn sheep imagery is as prevalent in the Southwest as the animals themselves once were. Their presence indicates the strong ties ancient hunter-gatherer cultures had with this hearty desert dweller. Evidence of this relationship is found in the material culture. Among the artifacts are cloaks, headdresses, hoof rattles, and horn ladles. Bighorn sheep were apparently highly regarded. The Numic-speaking Paiute people of southeastern California associated bighorn sheep with rain, the animal serving as the shamans' helpers. Athabascans, such as today's Navajo use the ground horn as a medicine to strengthen their domestic flocks. Bighorn sheep disappear from the rock faces following the introduction of agriculture.

Bighorn Sheep, petroglyphs, Basketmaker Culture, BLM, Utah.

PHOTO ©BRUCE HUCKO

OPPOSITE: Hunting Panel, petroglyphs, Fremont Culture, BLM, Utah.
PHOTO ©BRUCE HUCKO

STONE WONDER
—Part Three—

THE DESCENDING CALL OF A CANYON WREN AWAKENS ME. I've been lulled to sleep by the quiet comfort of this place. And so have the voices. There is room for my own thoughts. Rock art tickles my mind. These images suggest patience. They puzzle me. Who is looking at whom?

Everyone brings to the land their own experience and, in turn, offers what every mark on stone does—another way of seeing, another way of thinking. Rock art invites diversity of thought, and perhaps that is its greatest gift. It can bring an understanding from us that longs for release. Today that message seems to be, "Look around you. Cherish your surroundings."

I gaze across the landscape. It is beautiful here, the location inspiring. The round buttresses of slickrock dive into the west, forming a thousand-foot cliff. A gentle slope of stone, dirt, and canyons rises up from its base and reaches into the horizon. Dense canyon shadows hide a thousand stories. These visual images encourage all my senses: to perceive more actively the world around me; to listen; to feel the sand, the heat, the cold; to taste the wild that still remains.

My view circles back to this mural of stone. The figures are fused ever more strongly to the stone by the sharpness and clarity of low angled light. The images carved here, like those who made them, like I hope to become, seem one with the land. Rock art completes the composition of the landscape and helps define what poet Eric Walter calls "the logic of broken country."

The entire Southwest is one great gallery of art extending from whatever panel you happen to be viewing off into all directions and unknown realms of the imagination. Several lifetimes of images await. Most I will never see, and that is fine with me. But what of this one? If I enter into a relationship with these "long-ago people to whom I am still related," what responsibilities do I bear? Excited by what we see, do we swear ourselves to secrecy? A few friends will see photographs. With a few I may return. But in general I'll keep it to myself. Protecting the location of a site helps protect its mystery too.

I leave the rock face and begin my descent, careful not to leave many footprints. Let the next person have the same joy of discovery. Mind and spirit refreshed, as if a cool breeze swept through me, I playfully hop down the rocks to my pack. As I do, I stop and turn. The panel is lost in shadow. I did not discover this panel today. It revealed itself to me. A few paces into the canyon I pause for one last look. What's that I hear? Voices in stone? It's the rocks, laughing.

Masks, mask-wearing figures, and stylized faces may symbolize man's relationship with the sacred world. They enter rock art iconography after AD 1200-1300, and it is generally agreed that they represent the katsinas —supernatural beings that control particular natural phenomena. This belief system is still active among the Pueblo, Hopi, and other tribes. In today's ceremonies, masked members of the community impersonate the katsinas as they request rain and call for general well-being. All contemporary cultures in the Southwest employ masks and masked figures in their ceremonial calendars.

OPPOSITE: Five Faces, pictographs, Pueblo II-III Culture, Canyonlands National Park, Utah.
PHOTO ©BRUCE HUCKO

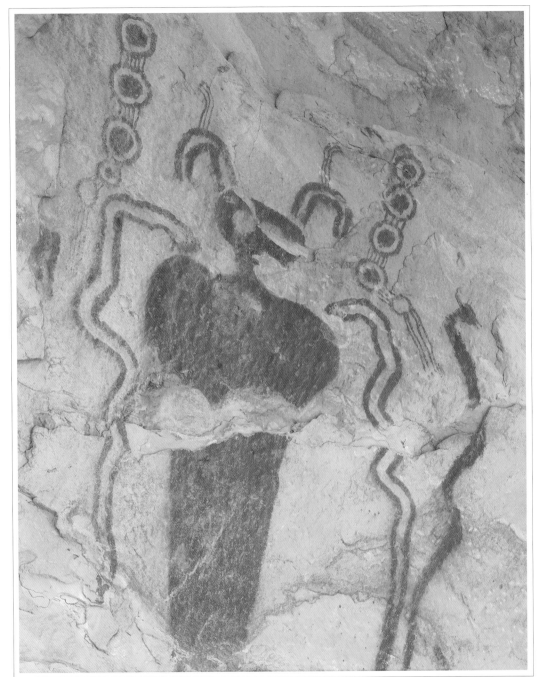

Shamans are present in cultures throughout the world. The overall task of the shaman is to maintain the balance between universal forces and people for community well-being. As specialists in the sacred they are able to call upon the powers of animal helpers, to see spirits, and to visit the gods by traveling to other spiritual dimensions.

Certain rock art imagery indicates the presence of shamanism in Fremont, Basketmaker, and other hunter/gatherer cultures. Horned headdresses, masked faces, elaborate dress, skeletal body forms, and the presence of animal "spirit guides" suggest a site was used for or recorded a shaman's ceremony or vision.

Sego Shaman, pictograph, Archaic Culture–Barrier Canyon Style, BLM, Utah.

PHOTO ©BRUCE HUCKO

Panel of shamanic pictographs, Basketmaker Culture, northern Arizona.

One White Hand, pictograph, Pueblo II-III Culture, Canyonlands National Park, Utah.

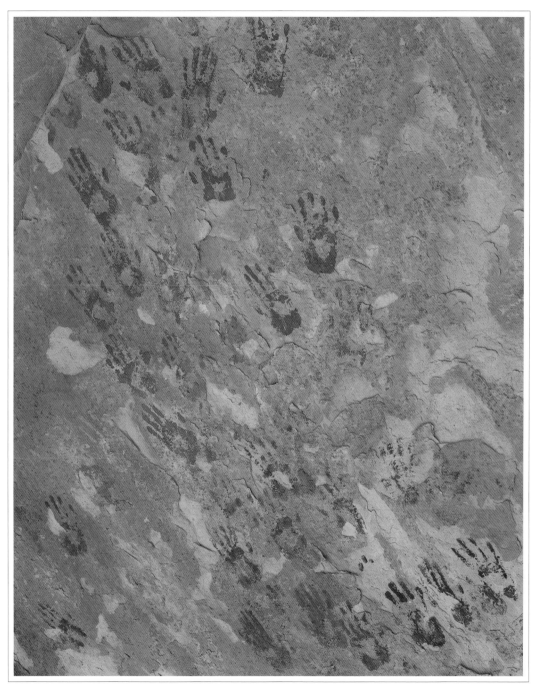

Many Hands, pictographs, Pueblo II-III Culture, BLM, Utah.

PHOTO ©BRUCE HUCKO

Applause or signature? Hand-prints occur throughout the Southwest and are a ubiquitous aspect of the pre-Puebloan Basketmaker culture. Most are painted and lifesize, though smaller hands and footprints occur occasionally. Most are made by dipping the hand in pigment (usually hematite,red) and then pressing it onto the rock. Sometimes a straight or zig-zag line pattern is drawn on the palm first. Another method is to hold the hand against the stone and then spray pigment from the mouth creating a reverse imprint effect. Hands are usually found in groups of less than two dozen. Some sites, however, contain more than 100 handprints.

Dating rock art sites is integral to the study of ancient cultures. Several controlled dating techniques are used to do this. The first is the physical association of rock art with other datable elements, such as building timbers, vegetal materials, nearby soils, and pottery. New methods of dating glyphs by measuring the age of the patina are underway. Light-colored petroglyphs are younger than darker, more patinated ones. Attempts to measure dates using the actual pigments are difficult and destructive. Only through dating can associations among rock art, building site, and material culture be accurately made and their uses and meanings inferred.

Lichen-encrusted bighorn petroglyphs, Basketmaker Culture, northern Arizona.

PHOTO ©JEFF D. NICHOLAS

Pictograph and granary, Basketmaker and Pueblo II-III Cultures, Natural Bridges National Monument, Utah.

Anthropomorphic figures, petroglyphs, Petrified Forest National Park, Arizona.

PHOTO ©JEFF D. NICHOLAS

The presence of humanlike imagery, referred to as anthropomorphs, delights and enthralls rock art viewers of all ages. Pervasive for 2,000 years this art form was practiced by Archaic, Ancestral and historic Puebloans, and the Fremont Culture. Anthropomorphs frequently appear in rows or clusters high above the ground, which gives them a supernatural aura. Bodies are often lifesize, decorated, with headdresses, and are shown holding or are in proximity to plants, animals, shields, and geometric forms. It is generally speculated that they were used as a religious storytelling device. Seen from a canyon trail they command attention and imagination.

OPPOSITE: Great Gallery figures, pictographs, Archaic Culture–Barrier Canyon Style, Canyonlands National Park, Utah. PHOTO ©BRUCE HUCKO

FRONT COVER: Holy Ghost Panel, pictographs, Great Gallery, Archaic Culture–Barrier Canyon Style, Canyonlands National Park, Utah. PHOTO ©BRUCE HUCKO

PAGE 1: Bighorn petroglyphs, Basketmaker Culture, Monument Valley Navajo Tribal Park, Arizona. PHOTO ©BRUCE HUCKO

FRONTISPIECE: Handprints, pictographs, Basketmaker Culture, Natural Bridges National Monument, Utah. PHOTO ©D.A. HORCHNER

TITLE PAGE: Anthropomorphs, petroglyphs, Fremont Culture–Classic Vernal Style, Ashley NF, Utah. PHOTO ©BRUCE HUCKO

BACK COVER: Galisteo Figures, petroglyphs, Pueblo IV Culture, New Mexico. PHOTO ©BRUCE HUCKO

ISBN 10: 1-58071-002-6
ISBN 13: 978-1-58071-002-2

Copyright 2008 by:
SIERRA PRESS
4988 Gold Leaf Drive
Mariposa, CA 95338
E-mail: siepress@sti.net
Sierra Press is an imprint of Panorama International Productions, Inc.

Printed in Singapore. First printing, Spring 1999.
Revised edition printed, Winter 2008.

PRODUCTION CREDITS

Series Editor-in-Chief: Jeff Nicholas
Book Design: Jeff Nicholas
Editor: Nicky Leach
Photo Editors: Jeff Nicholas and Laura Bucknall
Production Assistant: Laura Bucknall
Printing coordination: TWP America, Inc.

SIERRA PRESS
VISIT OUR WEBSITE:
www.NationalParksUSA.com

ARCHAEOLOGICAL RESOURCES PROTECTION ACT of 1979

Section 2(b) The purpose of this Act is to secure, for the present and future benefit of the American people, the protection of archaeological resources and sites which are on public lands and Indian lands...

Section 6(a) No person may excavate, remove, damage, or otherwise alter or deface any archaeological resource located on public lands or Indian lands...

(b) No person may sell, purchase, exchange, transport, receive, or offer to sell, purchase, or exchange any archaeological resource if such resource was excavated or removed from public lands or Indian lands...

(c) No person may sell, purchase, exchange, transport, receive, or offer to sell, purchase, or exchange, in interstate or foreign commerce, any archaeological resource excavated, removed, sold, purchased, exchanged, transported, or received in violation of any provision, rule, regulation, ordinance, or permit in effect under State or local law.

SUGGESTED READING ON AMERICAN INDIAN ROCK ART

Grant, Campbell, *ROCK ART OF THE AMERICAN INDIAN*, Dillon, Colorado: Vistabooks, 1992.

Hirschmann, Fred, and Thybony, Scott, *ROCK ART OF THE AMERICAN SOUTHWEST*, Portland, Oregon: Graphic Arts Center Publishing Company, 1994.

Muench, David, and Schaafsma, Polly, *IMAGES IN STONE*, San Francisco, California: Brown Trout Publishers, Inc., 1992.

Patterson, Alex, *A FIELD GUIDE TO ROCK ART SYMBOLS OF THE GREATER SOUTHWEST*, Boulder, Colorado: Johnson Printing Company, 1992.

Schaafsma, Polly, *INDIAN ROCK ART OF THE SOUTHWEST*, Santa Fe, New Mexico: School of American Research, 1980.

Schaafsma, Polly, *ROCK ART IN NEW MEXICO*, Santa Fe, New Mexico: Museum of New Mexico Press, 1992.

Schaafsma, Polly, *THE ROCK ART OF UTAH*, Salt Lake City, Utah: University of Utah Press, 1994.

A Case of
Red Herrings
Solving Mysteries through Critical Questioning

Book A2

THOMAS CAMILLI

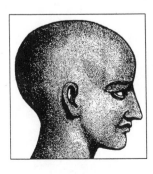

© 1993
CRITICAL THINKING BOOKS & SOFTWARE
www.criticalthinking.com
P.O. Box 448 • Pacific Grove • CA 93950-0448
Phone 800-458-4849 • FAX 831-393-3277
ISBN 0-89455-483-2
Printed in the United States of America

About This Book

The activities in this book are designed to improve your students' problem solving skills and refine their ability to apply logical deductive reasoning. To accomplish these, students are given the opportunity to solve puzzling mysteries in much the same way as a real detective—by asking probing questions and forming conclusions based upon the answers.

These activities can also help to change the way your students think. For example, the solution to some of the mysteries may require students to alter stereotyped sex roles or recognize the multiple meanings of key words.

How It Works

Each of the "mysteries" on these pages is part of a longer untold story which is "behind the scenes." It is up to the students to deduce the rest of the story from clues derived from answers to their questions.

For example, the story behind the sentence, "If Leo had kept his hand down he might be a free man today," can eventually be revealed if enough questions are asked and the answers are used to form a mental image of the event.

It may take many questions over several days to finally reveal that Leo is a not-too-bright bank robber who incriminates himself at his trial by raising his hand when the prosecutor asks a witness, "Is the person who robbed the bank present in the courtroom today?"

The Rules of the Game

The rules for these activities are simple.

- Students must phrase their questions so that the answer is either yes or no.

- You should try to answer questions with only a yes or no (occasionally a *maybe* or *sometimes* can be given as an appropriate response).

- You may give hints to redirect thinking or stimulate new questions.

Behind the Scenes

The solutions to these mysteries are found at the back of this book. It is important to visualize the scenario of the mystery before you begin a questioning session. That way you can answer questions based upon your personal mental image of what has taken place. After visualizing the scene, you may find that you need to alter it slightly to suit your geographic locale or your students' cultural backgrounds.

Suggestions for Use

As a motivator or time filler: These detective mysteries can be used as five-minute warm-up or sponge activities to begin or end a class period.

As a cooperative activity: Students can be divided into teams. Limiting the number of questions that a team is allowed to ask keeps one group from dominating the session. Each team may ask only one question per round, and the questions may be asked only by the team's spokesperson.

©1993 Critical Thinking Press & Software   P.O. Box 448   Pacific Grove, CA 93950
(800) 458-4849

This helps to eliminate frivolous questions. (In fact, many students will learn quickly how to narrow the search for important clues by asking comprehensive questions.)

Another method for limiting questioning is to pass out coupons to the groups before each session. A coupon is collected before each question is answered. When the group runs out of coupons, the group is out of that questioning session.

As a writing activity: Questions may be submitted only in writing. Questions are read and answered at the beginning or end of class. To prevent students who already know the answer from spoiling the activity for others, possible solutions should also be submitted only in writing.

To develop critical listening skills: After a few practice rounds, a new rule could be imposed: repeat questions will not be answered. This causes students to listen more carefully to each other's questions and answers.

Critical listening and recall is improved if the students are allowed to remark (with a noise or a word) when a question is a repeat of one that has already been asked.

As a lesson in critical thinking: Like all good mystery stories, the ones in this book have vivid plots, settings, and characters. Questioning strategies can be improved by finding areas of the stories that have not been thoroughly addressed. By analyzing individual questions and suggesting ways to improve them, you can increase students' critical thinking ability.

Tips

- Limiting the number of questions allowed during a session tends to improve the quality of the questions.

- Choosing a student to present the story and answer the questions allows you to model inquiry techniques by taking an active part in the activity. Instead of simply describing how to formulate good questions, you can then guide the students by demonstrating higher level thinking and questioning techniques.

- It is important to summarize the clues that have already been discovered before continuing an interrupted questioning session. This refreshes students' memories and updates students who may have been absent during a questioning session. One of the best ways to do this is to ask the students what they remember about the story and what clues have already been revealed.

Using the Mystery Pages

The pages in this book are designed for multiple uses.

- Reproducing the mystery page on transparency material and using it every time the story is investigated helps students who have a limited auditory memory.

- Summarizing what the students already know about the mystery and writing it on the transparency will help those students with learning difficulties to continue to participate in the questioning activity.

- Letting everyone see the actual mystery message permits students to analyze the wording of the mystery for possible clues.

- Using the mystery page as a poster in your room will serve to remind you and your students of both the activity and the mystery in progress.

Using the Graphic Organizers

A variety of graphic organizers could be used to help students with the thinking process. Two are supplied with this text. Here are some ways that they can be used:

For cooperative learning: Before beginning the questioning session, each group receives one copy of the mystery story and a copy of the graphic organizers. Encourage them to use the graphic organizers to arrange a questioning strategy. At the end of the session the group members can map out on the organizer the direction in which the answers are leading and plan the next questioning strategies.

Modeling the thinking process: Using a transparency of Organizer #1, select a mystery and model the process of analyzing the story for clues. Are there any words in the story that could have multiple meanings? Are there any clues about the setting, characters, or action of the story? From the first reading of the mystery, what are some possible solutions?

Guided practice: Individually or in cooperative groups, students could use Organizer #1 to help them analyze the wording of a mystery story. They could contribute their ideas about the mystery before beginning the questioning session.

Summarizing: Organizer #2 can be used to list the clues that have been discovered from previous questioning sessions.

The Questioning Process

To give you a better understanding of how to use these mystery stories to develop critical thinking, here is an abbreviated script of a questioning session with a group of students.

The teacher in this example uses several strategies to get the students to think in new and different directions without giving away the premise of the story. You might want to use similar strategies with your students to get them back on track if they get stuck or start pursuing a nonproductive line of questioning.

Teacher: "We're going to try to solve a mystery today. I know the entire story behind this mystery, but I am only going to let you in on a small part of it to begin with. It will be up to you to figure out the rest of the story as a detective would, by asking good questions, listening carefully to the answers, and putting clues together to form a mental picture of what is happening.

"Here are some rules that must be followed. You may ask me any question as long as it is phrased so that my answer can be a yes or a no. Listen to the questions that others ask because you may pick up clues from my answers to their questions. Try not to repeat questions that others have already asked.

"I will attempt to answer your questions with only a yes or a no. Sometimes that is difficult to do, so I may give more than a one-word answer to some questions. Listen to the way that I answer yes or no. That may give you a clue to the solution of the mystery or help you phrase your next question.

"Do you understand the rules? If not, be sure to ask for an explanation. OK, here is the mystery story: (the teacher places the transparency of the story on the overhead). It reads, 'Although she was not an unusually large person, people were constantly amazed at what Livia weighed.'"

Student: "What do you mean? Who is she? Is she really a big person?"

Teacher: "That's what you are supposed to find out by asking questions. If you ask enough questions, you can find out exactly what is happening here. Try it. Remember, your questions must be phrased so that I can answer them with yes or no."

Student: "Who is she?"

Teacher: "I can't answer that question the way it is asked. Please rephrase the question so that I can answer it with a yes or a no."

Student: "Is she a person?"

Teacher: "Yes. That's a good question. Why do you think it is a good question?"

Student: "The word *she* could mean lots of things. It could stand for an animal, like a lioness. Sometimes ships are called she."

Student: "When the story says that people were constantly amazed at what she weighed, does that mean that she was a really large person?"

Teacher: "No one said that she was a large person. You have to listen carefully to the way the story is told for clues to the mystery. Now, how is the story worded? Read it carefully because every word counts."

Student: "How can she be a small person and still weigh a lot—enough that people were amazed at her?"

Teacher: "I can't answer until your thought is posed as a question."

Student: "Is she a weight lifter? Does she compete in the Olympics?"

Teacher: "That's two questions. I can only answer one at a time."

Student: "OK, is Livia a weight lifter?"

Teacher: "No."

Student: "Does this have anything to do with how many pounds she weighs?"

Teacher: "No. Good question."

Student: "Does weigh mean that she weighs things for other people, you know like a butcher weighs meat for other people?"

Teacher: "No."

Student: "Does she weigh big things, like trucks or elephants?"

Teacher: "No."

Student: "Does the word weigh have anything to do with finding the mass of an object?"

Teacher: "No. But why is that a good question?"

Student: "It eliminates a lot of things with just one question."

Student: "Is Livia a judge?"

Teacher: "Before I answer your question, what made you think of that?"

Student: "Well, judges sometimes have to weigh the evidence in a case to reach a decision."

Teacher: "That's good thinking. Another use for the work *weigh*. I'm sorry, but the answer is no. Did that question start any of you thinking in a different direction?"

Student: "Yes, it makes me see that words can have more than one meaning."

Student: "Would it help to know what Livia does for a living?"

Teacher: "Yes."

Student: "Does Livia drive a truck?"

Teacher: "No."

Student: "Is she an airline pilot?"

Teacher: "No. Can you think of some questions that could narrow down what she does without having to go through all the occupations in the world?"

Student: "Does she work indoors?"

Teacher: "That's a good question. It covers a whole group of occupations with one question. The answer is no."

Student: "Can we then assume that she works outdoors?"

Teacher: "A good detective never assumes anything. They question every assumption to get at the truth."

Student: "Does Livia work outdoors?"

Teacher: "Yes."

Student: "Does she work on land?"

Teacher: "No."

Student: "Does she work at sea?"

Teacher: "Yes."

Student: "Does she work on a ship?"

Teacher: "Yes."

Student: "Oh, I think I know the answer!"

Teacher: "If you think you know, ask a question that will help others to discover the answer."

Student: "Does Livia work mostly when the ship enters and leaves port?"

Teacher: "Yes."

Student: "Does the word *weigh* have something to do with a part of the ship?"

Teacher: "Yes. I think you are close to the solution. Ask another question"

Student: "Is Livia in charge of raising and lowering the anchor on a ship?"

Teacher: "Yes. That's it!"

Student: "Huh?"

Teacher: "Livia handles the controls that raise and lower the massive anchor on the ship. She weighs it. In this case, the word *weigh* means to raise something. Can you see how people would be constantly amazed at what Livia weighed?

"Now, do you think you understand how these mystery stories work? Well, here's another one for you to try to solve. If we don't have time to complete it today, we'll work on it when we have some time left over tomorrow or the next day."

Levels of Difficulty

The mystery stories in this book have been leveled according to the amount of difficulty students will have reaching the solution. The stories in the beginning of the book are easier for the average class to deduce than those farther back. The first two or three stories are excellent to use when modelling the questioning process needed to solve the remainder of the mysteries.

Many stories in the last third of this book are complicated and will require a much longer period of time to solve. You may have to give more clues and actively guide your students' thinking as they work through some of the more difficult mystery stories.

Extending Activities

After students have experience solving the mysteries in this book, ask them to create their own stories. Sources for story ideas are mystery programs on television and unusual stories from magazines, mystery novels, or the newspaper.

The best mysteries are those which contain words that have more than one meaning. For example, a *story* could be one floor in a tall building, or it could be a written or spoken composition. A *stroke* could have something to do with the brain, or it could be a term that describes a tennis or golf swing. Try to incorporate these kinds of words into the story.

1

Mystery Story: _____

_____

_____

Words in the story which have multiple meanings:

Word: _____ Meanings: _____

Word: _____ Meanings: _____

Word: _____ Meanings: _____

Word: _____ Meanings: _____

What clues can you find in the words of the mystery story?

Setting clues	Character clues	Action clues
_____	_____	_____
_____	_____	_____
_____	_____	_____
_____	_____	_____
_____	_____	_____
_____	_____	_____

Possible Solutions:

_____

_____

_____

_____

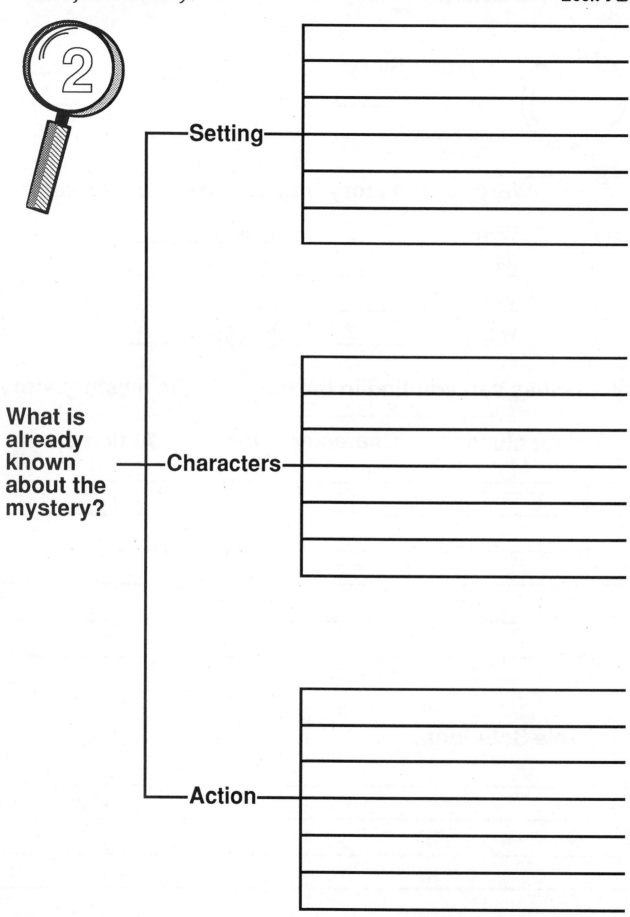

What is already known about the mystery?

Setting

Characters

Action

A husband and wife celebrated their 25th birthdays with their nine children, twenty grandchildren, and six great-grandchildren. How can that be?

Although she had lots of friends and had made millions of dollars during her long and successful career, Alise suddenly found herself alone and penniless. How can that be?

©1993 Critical Thinking Press & Software   P.O. Box 448   Pacific Grove, CA 93950
(800) 458-4849

A massive earthquake destroys a dam at the mouth of a huge reservoir. Although a large community is in the direct path of floodwaters, no homes are destroyed or people killed. How can that be?

If only she had seen the light, she might be free today. What happened?

©1993 Critical Thinking Press & Software   P.O. Box 448   Pacific Grove, CA 93950
(800) 458-4849

An inventor informed the press that he had devised a way to jump higher than the roof of his laboratory building without the aid of any mechanical device. When the news media arrived to document the event, they were surprised by what they saw. What was that?

While on an outing with some friends, twin sisters ate identical meals prepared by the same person. One of the twins remained perfectly healthy while the other became critically ill after the meal. Why?

The sign read, "We may be whipped, but we will never be beaten." Where is the sign, and what is meant by it?

©1993 Critical Thinking Press & Software   P.O. Box 448   Pacific Grove, CA 93950
(800) 458-4849

Although the woman deliberately jumped from the top of the tallest building in town, she was neither injured nor killed by the fall. How can that be?

Lavar knew that for what he had done, he would eventually have to face the music. Why?

It is found in England, France, Spain, and China, but not in Portugal, Italy, or Greece. What is it?

©1993 Critical Thinking Press & Software   P.O. Box 448   Pacific Grove, CA 93950
(800) 458-4849

The car traveled for nearly a mile with a flat tire, yet the driver was unaware of it. How can that be?

©1993 Critical Thinking Press & Software   P.O. Box 448   Pacific Grove, CA 93950
(800) 458-4849

Two identical containers are each filled with the same food, yet one container weighs substantially less than the other container. How can that be?

©1993 Critical Thinking Press & Software P.O. Box 448 Pacific Grove, CA 93950
(800) 458-4849

Working together, two shoplifters stole something from a store. As a result they each received six months for their crime. What did they steal?

Even though he made straight A's in school, Louis was not allowed to graduate with his class. Why?

"Sharks! Sharks!" shouted the lifeguard, but none of the swimmers seemed the least bit concerned for their safety. Why?

If she hadn't crossed the line, they might both be alive today. What happened?

A heavily armed man held up a series of bars, robbing onlookers of their gold and silver. Although many of the onlookers knew the identity of the man, the police were never notified of the incidents. Why?

A woman found herself jailed for stopping her car before turning right at a busy intersection. How can that be?

©1993 Critical Thinking Press & Software   P.O. Box 448   Pacific Grove, CA 93950
(800) 458-4849

Even though his face was completely masked throughout the robbery, police were waiting for him when he arrived at his home. How did they know?

The sign outside the business read, "Don't jump to conclusions. Take your time, pack carefully, and read and follow all directions." What was the business?

She had captivated the crowd with her performance, but she knew disenchantment would quickly follow the next strike. What is happening?

©1993 Critical Thinking Press & Software   P.O. Box 448   Pacific Grove, CA 93950
(800) 458-4849

Ludlow got detention for asking to have his spelling corrected. How can that be?

When they invented it,
they never realized how
many lives it would save.
What is it?

©1993 Critical Thinking Press & Software   P.O. Box 448   Pacific Grove, CA 93950
(800) 458-4849

I live in a strange town. The law states that no man may shave himself. Instead, every man must be shaved by the town barber. But there is only one barber in town. Who shaves the barber?

©1993 Critical Thinking Press & Software   P.O. Box 448   Pacific Grove, CA 93950
(800) 458-4849

While peeling potatoes for dinner, Mac accidentally cut his finger. Within a few minutes he was dead. What happened?

The headline read, "Woman Survives Twenty Story Fall." How could she have done that?

©1993 Critical Thinking Press & Software   P.O. Box 448   Pacific Grove, CA 93950
(800) 458-4849

After both engines failed, the pilot ordered the passengers and crew to bail out. Even though not a single parachute opened, they all survived the ordeal. How?

Taking advantage of a momentary distraction caused by her companions, she broke free from the guards and fled in a futile attempt to evade capture. Why was she being held?

Within the space of a week she had married and divorced two men and was engaged to marry another, yet those who knew her were not surprised by her actions. Why?

The headline read, "Unexpected Plant Closure Surprises Workers." What is the story about?

©1993 Critical Thinking Press & Software   P.O. Box 448   Pacific Grove, CA 93950
(800) 458-4849

Behind the Scenes

1. *A husband and wife celebrated their 25th birthdays with their nine children, twenty grandchildren, and six great-grandchildren. How can that be?*

The husband and wife were married to each other. They were both born on February 29, a leap day. Their birthdays technically happen only once every four years. Although they are both actually 100 years old, they are celebrating only their 25th birthdays.

2. *Although she had lots of friends and had made millions of dollars during her long and successful career, Alise suddenly found herself alone and penniless. How can that be?*

Alise found herself alone and penniless in her cell in a federal prison. As a skilled forger, she had literally "made" millions of dollars in counterfeit money and now was being punished for her crime.

3. *A massive earthquake destroys a dam at the mouth of a huge reservoir. Although a large community is in the direct path of floodwaters, no homes are destroyed or people killed. How can that be?*

The area had been suffering from a prolonged drought and as a result the reservoir was nearly empty when the dam collapsed.

4. *If only she had seen the light she might be free today. What happened?*

Driving through a residential neighborhood late at night, a woman was stopped by the police for driving with a broken headlight. A check revealed that the car she was driving was not hers. It had been stolen earlier in the day and used in a series of bank robberies and the woman had been the get-away driver. She was incarcerated for her crime.

5. *Jen told her friends that what she does for a living takes strength, skill, patience, determination, and lots of guts. What does she do?*

Jen strings tennis rackets for professional tennis players. The special string used on professional rackets is called gut.

6. *Although a wealthy woman, Elsa only made friends with the poor and destitute. Why?*

As a youngster, Elsa had heard the old saying that "a friend in need is a friend indeed." Being a literal thinker, she believed it and practiced it in her daily life.

7. *An inventor informed the press that he had devised a way to jump higher than the roof of his laboratory building without the aid of any mechanical device. When the news media arrived to document the event, they were surprised by what they saw. What was that?*

It had been a slow day. The inventor thought up a little joke to play on the media. It was easy for him to jump higher than the roof of his laboratory building since the roof of his laboratory building cannot jump at all. When the media arrived they were greeted by a sign describing the hoax.

8. *While on an outing with some friends, twin sisters ate identical meals prepared by the same person. One of the twins remained perfectly healthy while the other became critically ill after the meal. Why?*

The twins were attending a community gathering in a local park. They had been stopping at various booths to sample food. At one booth they purchased a meal of cooked meat strips on wooden skewers. Unknown to them, the cook was running out of bamboo skewers and was cooking some of the meat on skewers made from the branches of a nearby bush. The wood contained a powerful toxin. One of the twin's meals was skewered on bamboo while the other's was cooked on poisonous branches.

9. *The sign read, "We may be whipped, but we will never be beaten." Where is the sign, and what is meant by it?*

The sign is part of an advertising campaign for a very proud dairy company.

10. *Although the woman deliberately jumped from the top of the tallest building in town, she was neither injured nor killed by the fall. How can that be?*

Although she was neither injured nor killed by the fall, the woman *was* killed by the sudden stop at the end of the fall.

11. *Lavar knew that for what he had done, he would eventually have to face the music. Why?*

Lavar had recently graduated from a school of music and was embarking on a career as an orchestra conductor.

12. *It is found in England, France, Spain, and China, but not in Portugal, Italy, or Greece. What is it?*

It is the letter N. It is also found in Japan, Canada, and Denmark.

13. *The car traveled for nearly a mile with a flat tire, yet the driver was unaware of it. How can that be?*

The tire was on a new car that was being transported by truck, along with several other new cars, to an auto dealership.

14. *Two identical containers are each filled with the same food, yet one container weighs substantially less than the other container. How can that be?*

Both containers are filled with popcorn. One is filled with the dried popcorn kernels, and the other is filled with popped corn.

15. *Working together, two shoplifters stole something from a store. As a result they each received six months for their crime. What did they steal?*

A calendar.

16. *Even though he made straight A's in school, Louis was not allowed to graduate with his class. Why?*

Although Louis, a talented kindergarten student, made straight A's, his B's and C's were awful, and he didn't know how to write his other letters and numbers. As a result, he was required to repeat kindergarten.

17. *"Sharks! Sharks!" shouted the lifeguard, but none of the swimmers seemed the least bit concerned for their safety. Why?*

The Sharks, the name of the visiting water polo team, had just scored a goal. The lifeguard for the event, also acting as the referee, was verifying the score by shouting the scoring team's name to the scorekeepers over the din of the spectators.

18. *If she hadn't crossed the line, they might both be alive today. What happened?*

A metal circus tent pole was being erected with the help of one of the circus elephants when it touched a high voltage power line that was overhead. The surge of electricity killed the elephant whose body fell onto the trainer who was directing the activity, killing him.

19. *A heavily armed man held up a series of bars, robbing onlookers of their gold and silver. Although many of the onlookers knew the identity of the man, the police were never notified of the incidents. Why?*

The "heavily armed man" was a muscular weight lifter participating in the Olympics. His success at a variety of weight-lifting events (holding up several "bars") had robbed other contestants of their chance for gold or silver medals.

20. *A woman found herself jailed for stopping her car before turning right at a busy intersection. How can that be?*

The woman was playing Monopoly® with some friends. She rolled the dice and stopped her game marker—a little metal car—on the corner of the game board labeled "Go To Jail."

21. *Even though his face was completely*

masked throughout the robbery, police were waiting for him when he arrived at his home. How did they know?

The robber wore a motorcycle helmet with a face guard that completely masked his features. However, he had not remembered that his name was painted on the back of his helmet, which victims noted and reported to the police.

22. *The sign outside the business read, "Don't jump to conclusions. Take your time, pack carefully, and read and follow all directions." What was the business?*

A school for sky divers.

23. *She had captivated the crowd with her performance, but she knew disenchantment would quickly follow the next strike. What is happening?*

Cinderella is running away from the ball.

24. *Ludlow got detention for asking to have his spelling corrected. How can that be?*

Ludlow is a not-too-bright criminal. While at the post office one day admiring his photo on a wanted poster, he noticed that his name was misspelled. When he went to the counter to complain about the error, a plainclothes policeman waiting to mail a package became suspicious and detained Ludlow for questioning. He was subsequently arrested.

25. *When they invented it, they never realized how many lives it would save. What is it?*

The photograph.

26. *I live in a strange town. The law states that no man may shave himself. Instead, every man must be shaved by the town barber. But there is only one barber in town. Who shaves the barber?*

The barber is a woman, so she is allowed to shave herself.

27. *While peeling potatoes for dinner, Mac accidentally cut his finger. Within a few minutes he was dead. What happened?*

Mac was the cook aboard a ship steaming up a piranha-filled tributary of the Amazon River. Not thinking of where he was, Mac reached over the side of the boat, dipping his hand into the river to rinse the blood off. The ensuing piranha attack did the rest.

28. *The headline read, "Woman Survives Twenty Story Fall." How could she have done that?*

The woman was in an advertisement for an amusement park. The woman was riding an attraction that raised a passenger compartment 200 feet (20 stories) into the air then dropped it back to earth beneath a parachute.

29. *After both engines failed, the pilot ordered the passengers and crew to bail out. Even though not a single parachute opened, they all survived the ordeal. How?*

The pilot, a special type of ship captain, was guiding a ship through a storm-tossed channel when the ship's engine room flooded, causing the engines to quit and shutting down the bilge pump. The pilot ordered the passengers and crew to bail out the water from the engine room in order to restart the engines. Their actions were successful.

30. *Taking advantage of a momentary distraction caused by her companions, she broke free from the guards and fled in a futile attempt to evade capture. Why was she being held?*

She was the quarterback of a football team. With the help of her teammates, she broke free from the guards of the opposing team and unsuccessfully ran for the goal.

31. *Within the space of a week she had married and divorced two men and was engaged to marry another, yet those who knew her were not surprised by her actions. Why?*

As a judge, she has the power to marry people and grant divorces. This week had been particularly busy. She had already married two couples and granted two divorces, and was engaged to perform another marriage.

32. *The headline read, "Unexpected Plant Closure Surprises Workers." What is the story about?*

The story is about worker bees becoming trapped in a Venus flytrap, an insect-eating plant.

 ©1993 Critical Thinking Press & Software   P.O. Box 448   Pacific Grove, CA 93950
(800) 458-4849